How To Be Old

How To Be Old

The thinking person's guide to retirement

by

Marcus Tullius Cicero

Adapted by
Richard Gerberding

Illustrated by
Lance Rossi

qp

QUID PRO BOOKS

New Orleans, Louisiana

Published in 2014 by Quid Pro Books.

ISBN 978-1-61027-264-3 (pbk)

QUID PRO BOOKS

Quid Pro, LLC
5860 Citrus Blvd., Suite D-101
New Orleans, Louisiana 70123
www.quidprobooks.com

qp

Publisher's Cataloging-in-Publication

Cicero, Marcus Tullius.

How to be old : the thinking person's guide to retirement (a modern adaptation of Cicero's essay On Old Age [De Senectute], with commentary) / by Marcus Tullius Cicero; adapted by Richard Gerberding and illustrated by Lance Rossi.

p. cm. — (Journeys and memoirs)

Includes bibliographical references.

ISBN 978-1-61027-264-3 (paperback)

1. Old age. 2. Old age—early works to 1800. 3. Friendship. 4. Ethics, Ancient. I. Gerberding, Richard. II. Rossi, Lance. III. Title. IV. Series.

PA 6308 C2 G17 2014   2014542981

Second printing, Dec. 2014. Also available in ebook editions in leading formats, and a hardcover edition, ISBN 978-1-61027-267-4, from Quid Pro Books.

This book is lovingly dedicated to:

George Gerberding (age 92)
Dino Betti (age 82)
Richard Elkin (age 87)
Donald Engrebretson (age 97)
    and
Leni Spangenberg (age 90)

From them I have learned the
important things.

Thanks ...

In the preparation of a book, gratitude is due to many people. Let me publicly and from my heart thank two groups:

Andrew Dunar, Bryan Ward-Perkins, and Heidi Colsman-Freyberger who kindly read the manuscript in its entirety and saved me from much disgrace.

David, Matilde, Mical, and Gavriel Betti-Nelken who gave me food, shelter, love, and great encouragement during its writing.

Table of Contents

How To Be Old

Adaptor's Preface

"Getting old is not for sissies" – the mortal words of Bette Davis. What you have in your hands are the immortal words of Marcus Tullius Cicero on the same subject. Well, almost the same words; I have jacked some around a bit, deleted and added a few here and there to make him clearer to us non-Romans. Over two thousand years ago, the Roman statesman Cicero, or Old Tully as he was sometimes known in the nineteenth century, wrote a work called *On Old Age*. If he wrote it today, Revlon and Max Factor would buy up the rights and suppress it. But the Roman cosmetic merchants didn't, and Cicero's book has not only survived, but has been superbly edited and elegantly translated into most of our modern languages and so, of course, almost nobody reads it but academics.

About twenty-five years ago when my parents were retiring, Tully's tome on getting old was pressed into my none-too-eager hands by my Latin teacher. I read it, as most do, because I had to, but I was amazed and delighted by what I found. The book was my first brush with what I now know to be moral philosophy. This branch of philosophy is not the highly intellectual, rigorous (and often deathly dull) pursuit of the academic and professional thinker, but rather the serious consideration of the best way to live. Moral philosophy, thank goodness, is a healthy step above the "self-help books," but often has the same purpose. Marcus Cicero certainly knew how to live. He came from the hind foot of nowhere to become high society's most successful lawyer, was the most imitated writer in Latin, lived in the Beverly Hills or Chevy Chase of his day, had several charming second homes in the Italian countryside, and lived a daily routine full of servants, family, students, and admirers. At one point he was the elected head of the Roman state, which meant that he governed a huge foreign empire, and he was in debt up to his Roman ears. Nothing deathly dull here. He was known for his clear head, his eloquence, his high sense of duty, and his sense of humor, which also got him into trouble. Like many eloquent people, he often didn't know when to shut up. Tribonius, one of Caesar's henchmen, published a book of Cicero's jokes while Cicero was still alive.

It was probably fate and not coincidence that caused me to read Cicero's book at the same time as Mom and Dad retired, because I noticed that Tully's and middle-class Americans' approaches to old age were at odds. My parents moved mountains to deny that they were in the third stage of life, whereas Cicero points out its advantages and asks us to accept it as natural and good. For my parents and their friends, there was nothing natural or good about it. Out came the tennis shorts, the hair dye, the youthful Polo shirts. They bought speed boats. Some took up running, others skiing, even weight-lifting. Adolescent words fell awkwardly from their lips, words like "gang," "kids," "workout," "whatta blast!," and "oh, you're soooo tan." Their retirement activities seemed to be primarily ones of the body, not the mind. Snorkeling rather than art, architecture, or intelligent conversation seemed to represent the ideal pastime. Now some twenty-five years later as I face retirement myself, I listen in horror to my own mouth: "cool," "hang out," "awesome," and I read about lifts, tucks, and Botox.

It ain't for sissies, but I am convinced it is best lived as Tully advises, that is, accepting it as natural and exploiting its own natural advantages. Besides, your knees probably look as ridiculous as mine do below those tennis shorts.

So why should you read this version of *On Old Age* rather than the ones produced by professional classicists? Because here I have attempted not simply to translate the Latin (something which I did do) but to transpose and adapt his work to American surroundings. His ideas are so provocative, so wonderful, so helpful, so natural, and so reassuring that I found it a tragedy that they could be lost in translations whose purposes were linguistic accuracy rather than pertinence. I have tried to make him as relevant and as readable to modern American thinking men and women as he was to their ancient Roman counterparts. Exit all his references to obscure ancient generals and philosphers and enter Dwight Eisenhower and Irving Berlin. Cicero was not talking to those who do not think about what they do; the mindless went to gladiatorial games or to the racetrack. If Nascar is the center of your retirement, this book is not for you. But if you try to be aware of the world around you, enjoy intelligent conversation and worthwhile ideas, and want to be proud of the years you have earned, take Old Tully home with you, have a nice dinner, listen to him, and think very carefully about what he says. He will become as valued a friend of yours as he is of mine.

R. Gerberding
Bologna, Italy
June, 2014

How to Read This Book

This book is not for sissies: it contains the sort of serious thinking that has lasted for over two thousand years, but it takes mental effort to extract it. Cicero was aware of this and wrote with a style and clarity that would make the weight of his thoughts easier to bear. He did not write for philosophers but for us. When you read him, think. It is okay to lower the book, peer out over your glasses (probably bifocals like mine) and reflect on the two or three sentences you have just read. If you don't think as you read, you are likely to consider the first part of the book simply intelligent common sense and the last part, the sections about death and the immortality of the soul, as simply nicely worded piety. But they aren't. Every part of this book is important. There is very little fluff in here. There are only three structural elements: (1) very few words that establish the fictitious historical setting and dialogue, (2) his ideas, and (3) specific examples from history or literature that support the ideas. That's it. So again, it is okay to stop and ponder, and if what you read seems simplistic, it is okay to re-read it. Nobody has to know how long it took you to read a short book. He has much to say to us oldies, and one of the most valuable lessons for us is to consciously and actively engage our minds. Do mental push-ups, intellectual workouts. The intelligent reading of his book will serve very nicely as your time in the mental fitness center. But no slouching, otherwise you will miss his points.

Some of the ideas the book contains are Cicero's own, but a great many come from his careful reading and pondering of thinkers far older and more philosophically significant than he was. He acknowledges his debt to Plato, who lived three hundred years earlier than he did, and to two of Aristotle's students. Modern scholars have found his use of the writings of many others. In all of this you will note the lack of the imperative, he does not tell us what to do. He is far too genteel and his style far too elegant to address us with recipes for a good old age. You will not find "take daily one hour of vigorous walking, thirty minutes of cross-legged Buddhist meditation, two cups of unflavored yogurt, and mix gently." Rather than instruct us like sous-chefs or boy scouts, he presents examples and concepts and assumes that we are intelligent enough to draw the conclusions.

You will also note the happy lack of any sort of recommendation to introspection. He was not pondering the depths of his Roman navel, no matter how concave, and does not suggest that we should "find ourselves." He seems to know that we best care for our insides by focusing outwardly on deeds and worthwhile activities that benefit others. This is probably distressing news to us of the Woodstock generation – we who long thought that the parental wisdom of the ages came from The Mamas and the Papas. But listen to him.

Listen to him especially when he talks about nature. His central theme in this book is that nature is something wonderful, and old age is natural. By nature he does not only mean blue skies, wind-filled trees, rushing brooks, biking trails, or even discolored and spotty apples at the farmers' market. His Latin word *natura* is often a direct translation of the Greek word *physis*, the etymological origin of our word physics, that is, the underlying force or organizing principle of the universe. Thus when he talks about nature or calls something natural he does not simply mean the pretty surface that we see and enjoy on a beautiful day (although that certainly neither escapes him nor ceases to delight him) but the basic rules and structures of our lives and of the world we live in.

In the sixth chapter (book) of his *On The Republic*, in a part of that work now known as "The Dream of Scipio," in almost sci-fi fashion, Cicero lays out his view of eternity, the world, and the relation between the two. Again, it is based on much older, mostly Greek, thinking. But given the fact that his account itself is now over 2,000 years old, it is amazingly "scientific." He sees the universe comprised of planets, stars, a galaxy, sun, moon, and earth. He has God (for him, Jupiter) assign men to a physical body and then, if they have lived properly, take them up at death to an allotted spot in the Milky Way to live happily ever after. It is a cosmic view full of surprisingly accurate astronomy, religious moral imperatives, and a clear notion that the nature of the universe and human nature are parts of one sacred whole.

I have left the traditional paragraph numbers in brackets to facilitate reference to other translations or to Cicero's Latin original. Even if your high-school Latin seems as far away as the Romans themselves, armed with the paragraph number and with a translation, you may find that you gain insight from time to time by consulting Tully's original words. But you don't have to.

Cicero's book is an account of a dialogue at a fictional

dinner party supposedly having taken place some 130 years before he was writing. Dialogue was the standard format for ancient philosophical works, popular ever since the days of Plato. This format had young people ask questions of an older, wiser, primary character whose answers would lay out the author's important ideas. Cicero chose Cato as his primary interlocutor, who was questioned by two younger men, Laelius and Scipio. I set the fictional dinner party in 1987 at the home of Senator William Fulbright. In this American version, Senator Fulbright is questioned by the young couple David Eisenhower and his wife Julie Nixon.

Although Tully doesn't say so explicitly, he obviously thinks that we oldies should clearly recognize old age as the final stage of life and give up the considerations we had in the former stages with providing for the future. For us Americans, this is often a preoccupation, an obsession, with goals, objectives, deferred reinforcement, and planning. We worry about the future at the expense of the present. In his comments about miserliness and about learning, we can sense a subtle but important admonition to follow the Roman injunction, *carpe diem*, and cease the thought for tomorrow and begin to wring the natural advantages from today. Now there is a very real stress-reliever, if we can achieve it. He has a long list of real things for us to delight in during our retirement, so maybe we can.

This book is not an easy or a "fun" read. Even though Tully writes in an almost light and breezy conversational tone for his fictitious dinner party, his ideas are provocative and demand thought. They will stay with you and actually help in your "golden years." At least, they have helped me in mine.

A big part of the preparation of this book has been the search for modern characters familiar to us Americans to replace Cicero's ancient and often obscure ones. If you would like to see who has replaced whom, the list is at the end: The Cast of Characters, alphabetized by the modern stand-in. Check them out as you read. Some of the replacements are amazingly parallel, some stretched, some delightfully ridiculous. But all serve, I think, to heighten the relevance of what he says for us non-Romans.

And last, pass this book on to someone else, hopefully to someone young. But good luck with that.

The next words you will read are Tully's. He begins with the traditional purple patch dedicating the work to his best friend. I have done the same, substituting my best friend for his. Bear with him (us), after a few pyrotechnic paragraphs he gets onto the subject matter.

HOW TO BE OLD

Bridgeman,
Has earth anything to show so fair
As one who travels trestles and is there
In the final span of metaphor
When road slopes to opposing shore?

I am taking the liberty to address you, Curtis, with those words worthy of addressing the gracious and enduring qualities of Rome's skyline because I have often seen the European ideals of control and moderation reflected in you. Not only does your very Anglo-Saxon name come from there, but you also sport the gentility and good sense we both have long admired in European heroes. There are problems in both our lives, as there are in all lives, but consolation (or maybe commiseration) is not what I have in mind here. This is a book about old age.

[2] I hope writing about old age will make its burdens easier for both of us, writer and reader, burdens already beginning with me and ones which will (we

hope) someday confront you as well. Since you will probably take old age in stride, calmly and wisely as you do most things, you seemed to me the obvious one to whom I should dedicate this book. As I said, I hope it will benefit both of us, not only me the old, but also you the young. In fact, I have already benefited: simply collecting these ideas has lessened the irritations of my increasing antiquity and in many ways has actually made it pleasant. As you with your degree in philosophy know better than I do, serious and intelligent reasoning about the real things that confront us can never be praised enough, and, if we follow what we reason out, we can actually rid any stage of life of a lot of hassle. You and I will continue to solve the world's problems, but for now I will simply send you this on one of them: the problem of old age.

[3] This book is in the form of a philosophical dialogue, but I did not make my main character the ancient Roman, Marcus Cato, as Cicero did in the original, but I used a modern American, Senator William Fulbright, when he was an old man. This seemed to give the book's ideas more relevant authority than they would have coming from the lips of a dusty old Roman. I set the fictional scene on a supposed night in April of 1987 when Senator Fulbright invited the young Eisenhowers, David, the president's grandson, and his wife, Julie, President Nixon's daughter, to dinner, and we will watch them marvel at how easily the Senator carries his years. If the Senator seems here to be more

learned than he was on TV, attribute it to his passion for history and philosophy, subjects he always read and continued to read in his later life. What more should I say? Nothing. Let's listen to William Fulbright talk about old age.

[4] DAVID: Julie and I are honoured to be here, Senator. It is a real pleasure for us to actually be with you, someone whom we have long admired for your political acumen when in the thick of it, and now you seem to deal with retirement so easily when others find it so depressing. So many retired people act as if the cares of the world were not taken from their shoulders, but heaped onto them. If you can actually tell us in one evening, we would really like to know how you do it.

FULBRIGHT: David, you seem to admire something that is really not that difficult. Old age is in a sense not a special case. Someone who doesn't have much in the way of inner resources will find all stages of life irksome, but someone whose character is in order will accept what nature brings and not complain about something perfectly natural, calling it evil. There is much nonsense bandied about old age, something which everyone wishes to reach, but which most complain about once they get there. That seems more than slightly inconsistent and perverse, doesn't it? They also say old age creeps up on us more quickly than we thought it would. But tell me, just how does old age creep up on middle age any more quickly than middle age creeps up on youth? The length of time before the onset of old age is not the issue here. To those who think it is, a life in their 800th year would be just as bothersome as one in their 80th. No matter how long the past lasts, once it has gone, it is gone, and a past that has no other virtue than its length will offer no consolation for old age.

[5] You are terribly flattering to say that you admire me and want to hear my thoughts. If I am at all deserving of your kind admiration, it is because I hold this one basic principle: the thinking person follows nature; nature is my guide. You can, if you wish, take nature as your guide because you see what is natural as having been instituted by God. But you don't have to; nature as physics does just fine. It is not likely that nature would wonderfully plan the earlier roles in the drama of life and then neglect the final act as some playwright who ran out of steam. How silly. Since all life in nature is mortal, there must be an end to ours too. Just as berries, grain, and the fruit of the land ripen and fall with a natural maturity, so too does the thinking person live

this maturity with calm and natural good sense. This is the heart of it all, for unless you accept this, you are fighting against nature, or if you wish, against God.

JULIE: Senator, I knew this would be good and I know I speak for David too when I say you would do us both a great favor if you could be more specific, especially about what you think we should do in our younger years to make our older ones as wonderful as yours.

FULBRIGHT: I will be happy to go on, if you young folk are sure you won't be bored.

JULIE: Heavens no! What a chance for us. It is like getting a map for a long road which we are about to drive from someone who has driven it.

FULBRIGHT: [7] All right then, Julie, I shall do what I can. You know we former senators still like to meet in the Senate Dining Room – birds of a feather, I guess. But I get a little tired of Illinois' Percy or old George McGovern griping about being old. They are almost as old as I am and they complain that the physical plea- sures have deserted them – too tired, too many doctor's rules – and that people who used to seek them out now ignore them. But they are angry at the wrong thing. If those complaints actually resulted from old age it- self, then all older people would suffer from them. But I know many people my age who are both happy to have the chains of physical desire slackened and who are not ignored at all by other people. Forgive me, but it is fairly obvious that the root of these complaints is not the age of the person but her or his character. Self-controlled and cultivated seniors live a good old age; rudeness and incivility are annoying at any stage of life.

JULIE: [8] I take your point, Senator, but, if you will permit me, that may be easy for you to say because of your wonderful reputation, respect, and privileged economic position. Not many people enjoy these advantages for their old age.

FULBRIGHT: There is a lot in what you say, Julie, but it doesn't cover it all. I remember a heated exchange once between Averell Harriman, who came from a New York family with bags of old money, and some whipper-snapper reporter from Ohio. The Buckeye blurted that the governor owed his national reputation not to his own ability but to the fact that he was a rich man from New York. Harriman, sometimes a bit of a haughty fellow, snapped back that even if he were the one from Ohio and the impolite reporter the one with money from New York, the reporter would still never amount to a hill of beans. The same can be said of old age. Yes, even the thinking person, if poor, will find old age difficult, but fame and riches will do nothing to lighten old age for those who do not think. [9] I tell you young people directly that the best weapons against old age are your inner qualities, those virtues which you have cultivated at every stage of your lives and which, after you have lived long and well, render the fruits of mature life really quite marvellous. This happens because of two things: (1) because the good qualities that are in you never desert you, and certainly not in the final stage of life, and that is wonderful, and (2) because the consciousness of a life well led and the recollection of many deeds well done constitute a most pleasant and reassuring memory, and this, of course, is only available in old age once you have accomplished those deeds.

[10] When I was a youth at Oxford, I began to worship Winston Churchill, Britain's later savior in World War II. He had a dignity and a flare about him that did not change at all in his later years. When I first took serious note of him, he was in his 50s, not that old, but old enough to me. I can list many outstanding traits in that man, but I don't think any are more impressive than the way he bore the death of his daughter, Marigold, who died in infancy. The letters he wrote about the loss to Clementine, his wife, were not only beautiful in style but the sentiments they contained would put profes-

sional poets to shame. You know, he was not only great in public when in view of his fellow citizens, but here was a man even more admirable within and at home. What style! What values! He knew his history and his Bible. For a practical politician, he was immensely literate. And what a memory! He could recall it all, not just British facts and figures but foreign ones as well. I was enthralled by him every time I heard him, and it was almost as if I predicted what eventually did come about: that after he died there would never again be someone from whom I would learn so much.

[13] Why am I talking so much about Winston Churchill? Well, because there isn't any way to call his old age wretched. Now, as you pointed out, we can't all be famous prime ministers who can recall winning important battles on land and sea and saving Europe in the process. But even the quiet life led honestly and with discrimination can lead to a peaceful old age. The examples here are legion; you know the famous ones. Plato died while writing – he was eighty. Robert Frost prepared a new poem for John Kennedy's inauguration in '61 when he was 87 and then went on to visit Khrushchev in the Soviet Union. Grandma Moses started, yes started, painting when she was seventy-five and lived to be one hundred and one. And she, when once asked why she kept painting so long, answered that if she hadn't taken up painting, she would probably raise chickens. She listed no complaints. Now that

is a wonderful answer and worthy of a thinking person, whereas an unreflective one would blame old age for what are really her or his own vices and faults.

[15] I have given some thought to this blaming of old age and I think it suffers four major accusations:

It keeps us from holding any kind of important position.
It makes the body weaker.
It deprives us of almost all of the pleasures.
It is the part of life closest to death.

If you would like to, we can take a look at each of these to see if they stand up.

THEY SAY OLD AGE KEEPS US FROM HOLDING IMPORTANT POSITIONS

FULBRIGHT: From which positions? I ask you. From those which are accomplished by youth and vigor. But there are the types of jobs done by the mind, even with less powerful bodies. Therefore did Churchill do nothing? David Eisenhower, did your grandfather, do nothing when still president at age 70? The other old men, your grandfather's secretary of state, John Foster Dulles and our current President Reagan, when they defended our rights and freedoms with their advice and authority, did they do nothing?

[17] The arguments of those who think old age keeps us from real and active contributions just don't hold water. Think of it like the running of a ship. There are the young sailors who load the stores, run the davits, move the heavy deck equipment around, fix the engines, swab and clean, and then there is the captain who sits quietly on the ship's bridge directing its course

and its operations. He does not do the things the young do, but what he does do is far more important. The really important things are always accomplished not by the strength or agility of the body but by deliberation, influence, and judgment, and these things are not taken from us in old age, but actually increase.

[18] Now if by chance I, who have been a Rhodes Scholar, a university president, and a US Senator, seem to have stopped being active now that I am retired, let me assure you it is not the case. My days are full and not full of "keeping busy." I use the influence and contacts I have gained with my years to get measures I think are important in front of members of Congress and maybe even more importantly, I constantly do what I can to keep this wonderful country aware of the threat posed by the Soviet Union. [19] Maybe someday, young Eisenhowers, you will be able to reduce that horrible threat. David, your grandfather saw it coming years ago and did marvellous things to keep Kruschev at bay. It hardly seems possible that Ike has been dead now for 17 years. Now there was a man who knew how

to handle his senior years. He certainly did not base his sense of self-worth on any youthful bodily strength – no skiing, tennis shorts, or mountain climbing for him. He is a real hero whose memory will not fade from the American heart and he gained that position by deliberation, reason, and judgment. Did you know that the words "*sen*ior" and "*sen*ate" have the same root? That is why our founding fathers named our highest legislative body the US Senate. [20] In fact, from reading history, something I love to do, and from, I guess, having been a small part of history myself, it is my conclusion that states often get themselves in trouble when they fall to the leadership of the young, and equally are often restored and run well when the old are in charge. I am reminded of Tennyson:

> A sober man, among his boys,
> Whose youth was full of foolish noise.

Foolhardiness is a trait of the age when we are flowering, prudence comes with growing old.

[21] You hear a lot about how the memory grows weak. No doubt it will if you don't exercise it or if you are by nature rather slow. But it doesn't have to. Old Averell Harriman knew the names of all he met and he never got one wrong. I don't fear I will lose my memory; reading helps a lot because it makes you recall things. I have never heard of any old people forgetting where they put their money. They remember what interests them: engagements, who owes them money, and what they owe. [22] What about our lawyers, preachers, teachers, and professors as old? Man alive, the things they remember! The faculties remain for seniors provided that their enthusiasm and activity remain – and that is not just true for the famous and powerful but also for those in private and peaceful lives. There is that great story about the ancient Greek playwright Sophocles who wrote tragedies until the ripest old age. He was such an avid writer that he seemed derelict in his family responsibilities and so his sons took him to court to get him declared incompetent by way of dementia. At the hearing, the old man recited a bit of his play "Oedipus Coloneus," which he was working on, to the judges and then asked if that seemed the work of a demented man. His sons lost the case. [23] The list of old people who do not at all lose their memory or their faculties is a very long one, and these names are certainly on it: Frank Lloyd Wright, Robert Frost, Albert Einstein, Grandma Moses, Thomas Jefferson, Immanuel Kant, and Ghandi. Did old age make these people dull in their pursuits or did their pursuits go sharply on,

lasting their whole lives?

[24] But for heaven's sake, we are not limited to famous people whose important work provides for the future. I can name you farmers from the hills of Arkansas, neighbors and relatives of mine, who go right on doing the everyday tasks: sowing, harvesting, and storing the crops. These are not things which gain lasting fame so why do they go on? First, people are never so old that they don't think they have at least one more year in them. Second, because thinking people, no matter what their way of life, see the lasting purpose in what they do.

One day the French Marshall Lyautey responded to his gardener who was complaining that the tree he had told him to plant would not mature for a hundred years:

> "In that case there is no time to lose.
> Plant it this afternoon!"

Or so said our President Kennedy about him. If you were to ask these people why they plant things they may not live to harvest, they will not hesitate to answer that God not only handed them the land from their ancestors but expects them to pass it on to the coming generations. They work for the future just as our national figures do. Shakespeare has a host of old kings planning for the next generation. But then, if you can believe it, he also has Albany say of the dead Lear when talking about suffering:

"The oldest hath borne the most."

I would counter that the old have also borne many things that are wonderful. I mean, even young people run into things they don't like to see. The Bard can get even worse about old age:

"Age, I do abhore thee."

[26] Attractive rather than abhorrent, I would say. For just as we old folk are delighted when you nice young people seek us out and show that you respect us, so too do young people like to learn about life and how to live it from the old. This evening is turning out to be pleasant for me and I hope for you as well. I hope you see

that old age is not at all languid and inactive, but that it is full and carries on many of the same things done in the earlier stages of life. In fact, many in retirement go beyond what they did before and learn new things. You know the saying from the ancient Greek, Solon, who declared he became old learning something new every day. For him poetry became a delight; for me, reading. In fact, I have taken it up so avidly that it is like satisfying some life-long thirst. Many of the examples I am citing to you now I learned in my retirement.

18

THEY SAY OLD AGE MAKES
THE BODY WEAKER

FULBRIGHT: [27] Yes, it does, but I no more miss the vigor of the young man than the young man bemoans the fact that he does not have the vigor of a bull or an elephant. You use what you have and gauge your activities accordingly. I remember that awful comment by the body-builder, Charles Atlas, when watching the young athletes warming up on the field. He then looked at his own old body and said, "You know, when I look at those guys down there I realize that these old muscles of mine are already dead." Well, it was not so much his muscles that were dead as the old fool himself, because he never went beyond the triumphs of his younger days which were all due to his body-building. But look what happens when you leave youthful activities to the young, not just in fact, but in your mind, and do what is naturally fitting for your age. Look at Supreme Court Justice Hugo Black or earlier at John Marshall, or more recently at William O. Douglas who all helped our Republic right to the end with their wisdom and their work in the law. They didn't consider themselves past it and already dead. [28] Even in my life, where giving speeches is so important, I used to fear that I would lose the necessary physical stamina. But the voice as it grows old actually gains some sort of resonant physical quality that is really quite splendid. I don't know what it is, but I haven't lost it, and you see my years. The speech and conversation fitting for an older person is quiet and relaxed, and often this elegant and soft style of speaking by thinking seniors in and of itself helps to make what they say more persuasive. If someday I get to the point where I no longer have the physical strength to speak in public, then I can teach the techniques to a Julie or a David Eisenhower. I mean, what can be happier than an old age surrounded by youth eager to learn?

[29] Speaking of teaching, here is something I think our seniors should do more of. We are the ones with experience and we should instruct and equip the young for their performance in all ways of life. Look

how happy your grandfather, the president, was made by the company of good young people. The loss of physical vigor does not lessen at all the satisfaction of teachers of worthwhile subjects. A weak body in old age is often brought about by our faults when we were young rather than by those of old age itself. A wild and lusty youth hands over to old age a body already worn out.

[30]   Sometimes old people don't sense a loss of strength at all. By golly, read the reports about our current president, Ronald Reagan. Despite that assassination attempt and now at age 76, he doesn't seem to sense any weakening of his physical strength. As a boy, I remember talk about the old pope, Leo XIII. He was elected pope at age 68 and held the office for 25 years! He was in such good shape that he never missed his youth. I could, I guess, say the same thing about me, after all, old men are allowed to talk about themselves.

[32]   Speaking of me, I am 83. I would like to be able to chop wood like Ronald Reagan does, but I can say

at least this much: admittedly I no longer have the strength that I had when I was president of the University of Arkansas but nonetheless, as you can see, old age has not really weakened me nor dragged me down. The Senate does not lack my advice, I still give public speeches, I am a consultant for Hogan and Hartson here in DC, and I keep up with friends and associates. I have never agreed with the old proverb that says, "If you want to be old for a long time, become old early." I was happy to get old when I did. Even if it means being an old man for less time, there is no need to rush it. And if you rush around being too busy to take time for people when you are young, they certainly are not going to seek you out when you are old.

[33] But getting back to physical qualities because they seem to be so important to seniors. True, I don't have the vigor of either of you two, but even you don't have the vigor of a Steve Reeves. Does that mean that he is more important than you? With physical ability, each age of life has to learn to control its desire for more of it and to attempt only what it can. That means you will not be shackled or frustrated by the desire for a body that you no longer have (or probably never really had). That body-building man, Charles Atlas, looks like he could carry a car on his shoulders. That would make a good half-time show in a stadium. If you could choose, would you rather be given that talent or, say, the vigor of intellect of a Thomas Jefferson? Finally, yes certainly, use and take care of your strong, young

body as long as you have it, but when it dwindles, don't long for it. This is not just true for seniors but for middle-aged people too, foolishly wracking themselves trying to be 20 again. The course of life is fixed, and nature has only one way; it assigns what is appropriate to each age. The weakness of children, the ferocity of youth, the weightiness of middle age, and the maturity of old age are true to nature, and each ought to be harvested in its own time.

[34] None of this is to say you ought to condemn yourself to an armchair. You know about old Strom Thurmond, a supporter of your father, Julie, and your grandfather, David. He is eighty-five and still gets around just fine, even in nasty Washington weather. He is healthy and does a bang-up job in the Senate. Appropriate exercise and moderation, therefore, are able to conserve something of our former physical vigor even in old age. And it is silly to think that old age has to be deprived of physical capacity and to treat seniors as incapable. By our rules and customs, older folk are relieved of obligations they can no longer perform and we are not forced to do what we cannot.

But sometimes this goes too far and people assume we cannot do what we in fact can. [35] It is said that the old are weak and they cannot perform the normal duties and responsibilities of life. But weakness is a property of ill health, not of old age, and any age can suffer ill health. David, the uncle you never knew, your Dad's older brother who died of scarlet fever at age three – if he had enjoyed good health he may have equalled your father or even his father, the president. It is no wonder that illness exists in the old if even the young are not able to escape it.

On the other hand, you must make a stand against the weaknesses of old age, David and Julie, which can be set right by constant attention. Fight against them as you would against disease. [36] You must pay attention to your health. You must exercise modestly and eat and drink to aid the body, not to burden it. And not just the body, but especially the mind and even more the spirit. Old age will extinguish these unless you give them fuel. Unlike the body, which you can ruin by overdoing it, the mind thrives by being pushed. The characters Shakespeare makes stupid old men in his plays are credulous, forgetful, and lazy. But these are not the faults of old age but of an inactive, cowardly, and sleepy old age. Just as insolence and lust are more characteristic of the young than of the old – but certainly not of all youth, just the morally lacking – so too is this geriatric stupidity, what we call our dotage, characteristic of frivolous old people, not of all. [37] Senator Al Gore's grandfather, Thomas Pryor Gore, had a comfortable estate, successful children, an enviable career as U.S. senator and lawyer – and all this as both blind and old. He had a mind that stretched like a bow and he never gave in to old age by becoming feeble. His prestige and his authority were felt by his associates, his children respected him, everybody (except maybe FDR and Co.) loved him. Traditional customs and learning were healthy in that house.

[38] When we retire, we generally retreat to more of a private and familial sphere, and here we will have an honorable retirement only if we defend it by our own right actions, if we keep our responsibilities and don't shirk them to others, and if we maintain our authority until our last breath. Just as we like to see a young

person in whom there is a bit of maturity, so too do we like to see an old one who retains some things of youth. Those who mix youth and maturity will be able to be old in body but never old at heart. I am now working on a new book I think I will call *The Price of Empire*.[1] I am doing the research, collecting the sources, finding things I have done and said, and polishing them a bit. I will comment on America's religious and cultural life along with, of course, foreign policy. I am using a lot of the history I have read in retirement. What I have worked on during the day I consciously recall and summarize in my mind before going to sleep. This is the workout for my memory, the laps for my mind. With this intellectual perspiration and working hard at these things, I do not miss the physical strength of my younger years.

As I said, I consult for my friends and get matters to the attention of the Senate. To both I often present briefs I have considered greatly and at length. All this

---

[1] J. William Fulbright and Seth P. Tillman, *The Price of Empire*, New York: Pantheon Books, 1989.

I do by the vigor of my mind, not my body. And when I can no longer do these things, then my reading chair will still be a delight as I think back on the things I have done. In these sorts of pursuits and labors, increasing old age is not really perceived. Little by little without our being aware of it, life grows old and so is not snapped suddenly, but simply fades out over a long period.

THEY SAY OLD AGE DEPRIVES US OF ALMOST ALL OF THE PLEASURES

Oh, this is a wonderful gift of old age, if it does indeed relieve us of most of the reasons youth gets itself into trouble. Remember, you young folks, the famous warning from Dr. Johnson, the especially great and famous eighteenth-century savant. I came to admire him when I was a young man at Oxford. He said that the body is all vice. The body's avid desire for the pleasures makes it seek them rashly and without control until it finds gratification. Oh the trouble! [40] These things often create traitors of their countries: they ruin governments and cause secret dealings with enemies. The desire for bodily pleasure drives people to commit debauchery, adultery, and crimes of all sorts. Since nature's (or God's) greatest gift to mankind is our reason, nothing is so harmful to God's gift than the desire for pleasure because it makes us act so irrationally. [41] By golly, when we are in hot pursuit of pleasure, there is no place for moderation or good sense. If the pleasure is too great and lasts too long, it will blot out any trace of rational thinking.

[42] Now why bring up this rather extreme notion? Well, simply to point out that if we cannot keep the desire for pleasure in bounds with our reason and good sense, then we should thank old age because it doesn't let loose things which are not fitting. The desire for pleasure may not extinguish all good sense, but it does impede good planning, provide all sorts of irrational reasons for doing stupid things, and, of course, it has absolutely no truck with virtue.

It was a real shame that the House had to censure Dan Crane and Gerry Studds. But I thought their licentiousness had to be officially branded. While they were serving in the House their deeds went undetected for a while, but Tip O'Neill rightly made them public. The things they did were bad enough as a private disgrace, but they were made much worse because of the abuse of Crane's and Studds' public authority. [43] There are many respected philosophers and theorists, Epicurus, Freud, and many Buddhist and Christian teachers, who point out the dangers of pleasure unleashed. In fact, remember how the British tried to promote the pleasures of opium in China in order to weaken the Chinese during the Boxer Rebellion? I sometimes wonder if those who devote themselves to the total denial of pleasure haven't thereby found something beautiful and taken up an enlightened goal very worthy of pursuit by the best of us. Although I would still opt for moderation rather than such an extreme.

[44] So why am I going on and on about pleasure? Because I want to impress upon you how the fact that old age is less subject to the passions for pleasure is not an indictment of this stage of life, but actually one of its greatest advantages. If it lacks all-night parties, or tables heaped high with rich food and powerful drink, it also lacks drunkenness, indigestion, insomnia, and "the morning after." It is not that old age lacks pleasures, it is that they change. And they are healthier. Gone are the overindulgent feasts and in their place we take pleasure in delightful dinner parties. Again, I am reminded of Churchill the war hero who was famous for his wit at dinner. He was of such a status that he could have live music and many official trappings even as a private citizen. [45] But again I don't have to talk about the world famous, I can provide personal examples. I have always had dinner parties, moder-

ate certainly, but not without fervor, which admittedly becomes tamer day by day as our age increases. And I never measure the pleasure of these gatherings by the opulence of the food and drink, but rather by the delightfully convivial discussions and conversations. In fact, "convivial" is the perfect word because it comes from the Latin, meaning "joined to life."

[46] Because of the delight in conversation, I enjoy long dinner parties, not just with my contemporaries, few of whom are left now, but also with people your age and with you. I feel grateful to old age, which has increased my enthusiasm for conversation, but let it wither for food and drink. Don't get me wrong, good food and good wine are still a delight: the pleasures, too, are a part of nature, and I don't declare war on them totally; we old folk do like them. But there are so many more pleasures at dinner: tasteful settings, a sense of occasion, the pleasurable American traditions set by our forefathers – turkey and cranberries at Thanksgiving, high round cakes at birthdays, Sunday dinners at noon instead of in the evening. We Ameri-

cans have a valuable set of table manners and rules for conversation over dinner, which if followed, provide real pleasure for all. They aren't necessary, but those different shaped glasses for different wines, the little ones for sipping liqueurs – all this contributes. Even eating on a cool porch in the summer or building a nice fire in the winter add real pleasure to the dinner. I do these things also when I am in Arkansas, away from DC, so almost daily I fill the dinner party with neighbours and friends and we stretch the time at the table into the evening with as varied a conversation as possible. Retirement is wonderful; I can do this much more often now.

[47] I agree, there is not so much "slap and tickle," as it were, among old people, but the great thing is that it is not even desired so much. The lack of something you do not desire is never noxious. Sophocles said it when a certain man asked him when he was old if he still enjoyed the pleasures of love. "Oh God protect us!," he said, "I run from them as if they were a fuzzy-mus-tachioed dictator." For those hot in the pursuit of the

carnal pleasures, not to have them is indeed tiresome and obnoxious, but for those satisfied and replete, it is more pleasant to lack them than to have them. [48] But even granted that youth enjoys these pleasures more fully, it enjoys petty things, and if old age does not participate in them much, it still doesn't entirely lack them. Just as those who have front-row seats delight the more in Ethel Merman's latest, those up in the balcony still enjoy the show. Thus youth, seeing the pleasures up close perhaps takes more joy in them, even old age seeing them from afar delights enough.

[49] Our old age has another wonderfully valuable characteristic: now the mind can retire in the true sense, that is, having already earned all the spoils of desire, of ambition, of struggles, of enmities, and of wants, it now, as the saying goes, lives for itself. "Been there, done that," as you young people would say. What a freedom! And, if our minds have been eager to learn something, nothing is more pleasurable than a retirement with enough leisure to pursue it. We have seen Billy Graham, close friend of your father, Julie, still pursuing his passion for evangelizing and writing, and he is now near 70.

[51] But just to show you that a pleasure of the mind does not have to come from books, let me mention gardening. What a delight this is for me, and it is one that is not at all impeded by old age Although gardening isn't very intellectual, it does come very close

to the life of a philosopher. Gardening is like having a bank account with the earth, one which never refuses to honor your drafts and which never returns what it has received without interest, sometimes with, alas, less profit, but sometimes with more. You know, it is not just the flowers or the fruits and vegetables that delight me, but it is watching the nature and the power of the earth. Earth first receives the seed in her soft and cultivated lap, she keeps it hidden, then she splits it open, keeping it warm with her own heat and compression. Then, from this, she brings out the first little green blade and it, supported by the fibers of the stem, grows little by little. Then you can see the joints in the stalk and when it is raised up a bit farther it enters, as it were, puberty, surrounding itself with sheaths. And from these comes the fruit.

[52] Grapes. I can go on forever about the planting, raising, and growing of vines. I cannot get my fill of them: the whole thing provides such peace and contentment in my old age. I am fascinated by the power of the earth, which takes a small seed like the fig or a

grape pit and produces such great trunks and branches. You cannot help but delight in admiration of the shoots, slips, cuttings, and layers. The vine is almost human: when it is about to fall to the ground, it grabs whatever it can with its tendrils as if they were hands, and raises itself back up. You have to know what you are doing in pruning it back so it doesn't crawl and spread everywhere and become too bushy. [53] The thing is so intelligent. In the spring, on the parts that remain, you can see at the joints what is called the bud, and, rising from it, the grapes themselves growing from the moisture of the earth and the warmth of the sun.

At first they are bitter to the taste, but then with maturity they become sweet. And this is really smart: because they are surrounded by the leaves of the vine, they retain warmth but are at the same time shielded from the damaging rays of the sun. Now I ask you, what is more enjoyable and beautiful to look at? It is not just the utility (that is the food and flowers) of the garden which delights me, but the process and nature herself. The stakes, the fitting of the cross pieces, the binding, fastening, the pruning of some, which I mentioned, and letting others run. Spading and watering to keep things fertile. [54] You want to hear about fertilizer? Probably not, even great authors often leave that out. But feeding plants is, I suppose, a way to compensate for no longer having children to feed while you wait for them to show up on visits. The lawn, meadow, vineyard, shrubbery, fruit trees, bees, and all the varieties of flowers provide real pleasure. And if you become very skilled, you can try your hand at grafting.

[55] All right. Enough. I don't want to bore you more than I already have. Forgive me for being so carried away by my love of gardening. I am aware that old age is rather talkative, lest I seem to excuse it from all its vices. But at some risk, I will say just one more thing. [56] Back to gardening, maybe gardening writ large, that is, farming. Our founding fathers were for the most part farmers. Managing his plantation was exactly what Washington was doing when word came that he had been chosen to lead the Continental Army. He and other founding fathers were summoned from their farms to national service. Is then a life lived close to the land a lowly thing? I would say the opposite, that is, it is hard to imagine a happier one, not only because of the great delight it gives in the processes of nature (or if you will, of God), as I have mentioned, but also because of its products. When we talk of what the land produces we are back to pleasure again. The wine cellar, the fridge, the larder of the good farmer

or gardener are usually full of wonderful things which everyone wants because of the pleasure they provide: meat, cheese, fresh milk, fruits, berries, vegetables, salad, even honey. Hunting, too, is a pleasurable activity that comes from the land, and game makes any meal more tasty.

[57] To sum up briefly. Digging in the dirt provides all sorts of pleasures. A nice green lawn, healthy trees and shrubs, flowers, plants, vines and fruit trees – nothing is more productive of good things nor more pleasurable to look at, and these qualities don't just interest us old folk, they positively allure us. And where, I ask you, can retirement better enjoy the warmth of sunshine, or the cool of shade or water than in the midst of well cared-for greenery? [58] Therefore let others keep their fast cars, speed boats, fitness centers, bats, rackets, and balls and leave us our checkers and bridge cards. But you know, they can take those too if we have a nice garden. [59] Franklin's Almanac is still a good thing to leaf through from time to time, and it is full of tips and praise for working the land. Sometimes it seems quite regal. Did you know that the word "paradise" is the Greek version of a Persian word meaning "walled garden"? Cyrus, the ancient Persian king of kings, is said to have delighted in laying out his gardens and even in planting things with his own hand. Enough.

[60] Let's talk now about the crowning pleasure of old age: this is really the respect and influence it enjoys. Retirement is the time of less work and more influence. I'm not talking about direct influence in your fomer work-place: that will cease; but of a more important type. To be influential in your later years you obviously need a bit of luck, but more so, you need sound character and virtue. [61] Old age, especially one which has been honoured by public office, has so much influence that it is of more value than all the pleasures of youth. [62] I hope you note in all I say, that the good old age I am talking about is one based on the foundations laid when we are young. I have said this before, and all agreed that an old age that has to defend itself with words is miserable. Neither grey hair nor wrinkles are suddenly able to snatch up respect, but rather the earlier stages of a life lived respectably are what produce the fruits of influence at the end. [63] There are small ways in which we Americans show this respect, and although they may seem common or even frivolous, they provide great satisfaction: to be recognized and

greeted when you are out and about, to be visited, for young people to stand up when you enter a room, to be consulted, or for those of us who have been in the public eye, to have a path made for you in crowds so you don't get jostled: these are types of things observed by well-mannered Americans and by thinking people in most other cultures. They mean a great deal. [64] How then can you compare the temporary pleasures of the body to lasting satisfaction of respect and influence? The seniors who enjoy them properly seem to me to have acted brilliantly through the drama of life and not to have collapsed in the final act, like some parvenu.

[65] But old people are often said to be peevish, finicky, easily provoked, difficult, even greedy. But these are shortcomings of character, not of old age. On the other hand, peevishness and the others I just mentioned do have something of an excuse, not altogether just, but understandable. Old people think that they are dismissed, ignored, and made fun of. Furthermore, in a fragile body every irritation becomes painful. Nonetheless, even these things are made easier by a sound character and worthwhile accomplishments. Take an example from the theater, which reflects life. In that new British play, "Blood Brothers," one brother is hard and nasty while the other is gentle and appealing. Not every wine grows sour with age, nor does every nature. I like a certain severity in old age, but as in all things, a moderate amount of it. Sourness, never.

And I certainly do not understand greed in the old. I mean, what is more ridiculous than laying in more provisions when less of the journey lies before you?

THEY SAY OLD AGE IS THE PART OF LIFE CLOSEST TO DEATH

FULBRIGHT: [66] This fourth accusation against old age, that the approach of death is probably not far from an old person, seems especially to trouble those in our stage of life. But misguided indeed is the one who does not see that death is not really something to be feared. Look at it this way. Either death extinguishes the spirit completely, in which case you can disregard it completely, or it leads the spirit somewhere better, and in this case death is actually something to be desired. These are the only two alternatives, there isn't a third option. [67] So where is the fear? With the first alternative my spirit will not suffer anything and with the second it will actually be happy. And another thing: nearness to death is not at all the exclusive property of old age. Old or young, who of us is so naïve as to think that it is somehow guaranteed that we shall live until dinner time? On the contrary, youth actually has many more causes of death than does our age. The young fall ill more easily, they haven't built up the immunities, they grow ill more seriously, and they have more fatal car accidents. Look at the war dead who were mostly young soldiers. The young are cured with more risk than the lucky ones who arrive at old age. And it is a very good thing that some do arrive, for as I said, intellect, reason, and deliberation are the properties of the old, and if there weren't any of us oldies around, then our institutions would be in trouble.

I'm wandering. I'll return to death as impending. What kind of accusation is it that old age is the time of impending death since, as you see, death is also very possible for the young? [68] I know this personally, I lost my father when he was only 52, just as you, David, lost your uncle. We all had the highest expectations for these fine young people. You and I both know very well that death is common to every stage of life. But, you say, that is not the point. The point is that a young person can reasonably hope to live a long time and an old one cannot. What an unwise hope. I mean, what is more foolish than to value uncertainty above certainty? Look at life this way, what the young person only hopes for (and the hope is uncertain, as we have seen), the old person already has. The one hopes to live a long time, the other has already done so. I already have memories, years, and life at a mature stage – all concrete things. The young only have hope for these things. [69] But my God, what does "a long time" mean? The longest lifetime, I suppose, we take from Methuselah in the Bible. Wasn't he supposed to have lived 969 years? But for me, any time which has a definite end to it (as life does) does not seem long-lasting, and once your end has arrived, then your past time disappears, leaving behind only your virtue and the good things you have done. These things are long-lasting; the span of your life is not. The hours, the days, months, even years pass. Past time never returns and we can't know what future time will bring. Time is not the important thing of life. We must take as enough whatever amount of time we are given for living. [70] To give a good performance, an actor does not have to appear in the last part of the movie: he can earn good reviews from what he does in any part of it. And neither must life be drawn out until some venerable time for the final curtain. A short time of life is enough to live well and honorably. If you do live longer, don't complain; farmers don't complain when the pleasantness of spring has passed, and summer and fall arrive. Spring is the time of growth, indicating the crops to come; the other seasons are designed for harvesting and gathering in the crops.[2]

[71] The "crops" of old age are, as I have, I guess, often said tonight, the good things you have done earlier and their memory. Everything produced according to nature, I think, should be considered something good. What then is more according to nature than for an old person to die? When death happens to the young, it is not natural: nature opposes and fights against it. When a young person dies, it seems to me to be like a vigorous flame being put out by a fire hose; with old people on the other hand, the flame is extinguished, having burned itself out on its own accord with no violent outside force. When unripe apples are plucked from trees it takes real force, but the mature and mellow ones fall gently and naturally. Violence carries life away from the young, from the old it is ripeness. And, you know, the ripeness is so pleasant to me that the nearer I approach death, the more I see it as land and that at last I am about to come into port after a long voyage. [72] There is, of course, no given time limit to old age. You will live well during it as long as you (1) accomplish the significant things you set out to, and at the same time (2) are not obsessed with death. These two things actually give the old more pluck and courage than the young. The best end to life is one where,

---

[2] Note that Cicero has old age as autumn, not winter, which would be more pessimistic.

with your mind and other senses still intact, nature herself dissolves what she has put together. Just as the same carpenter who has put a structure together can most easily take it apart, so nature who put mankind together is the optimal one to dissolve it. Every new construction comes apart with force, but the older one with ease. In the remaining time of life, let nature take its course. I cannot emphasize enough that we should not clutch at time unnaturally with strong medicines and machines, but by the same token we must never hurry the arrival of death by our own doing. The Bible tells you not to destroy yourself.

[73] There is a quote from the wise Solon where he says he doesn't want his death to lack grief and lamentation by his friends, I just think he wants to be dear to them. Mary Elizabeth Frye (who is now 82) says it more clearly:

> "Do not stand at my grave and weep;
> I am not there. I do not sleep."

[74] She obviously doesn't think that a death which is followed by immortality is something to be mourned. When we die, we do sense it, but only for a short time, especially if we are old. As I said, after death there are only two possibilities, either sensation of the spirit continues – and this would be a desirable thing – or it no longer exists. So either way, we should not be obsessed

with death. But learning not to fear death is something which must be continually practiced from youth onwards. Without this ability, no one can really have a tranquil spirit. I mean, death is certain, and it is also certain that it may happen at any moment, even today. So how can you live a tranquil life if you constantly fear an impending death? [75] I don't really need to dwell on this to make my point. We have a long list of proud Americans who led significant and even heroic lives without fearing death: Nathan Hale, who gave his famous "one life" liberating the fatherland; Glenn Miller, who got on that plane in order to keep his promise; your grandfather, President Eisenhower, who was a military man most of his professional life. And then, of course, our ordinary American soldiers who with courage and vigor marched into places like Iwo Jima even though they knew they would probably never return. With all these examples, isn't it silly if we educated old people fear that thing which even simple and uneducated young people can disregard?

[76] Then too, I think I can safely say that when the point arrives where you have had enough of life's pursuits – this isn't boredom but more a fullness or satisfaction – then you have also had enough of life. There are certain pursuits of childhood which teenagers don't miss, do they? And stable, middle-aged adults don't go running after the pursuits of teens, do they? And there are some interests of our middle years that we no

longer want when we are old. We old people have our own natural interests. Therefore, just as we do not fear or regret when the pursuits of earlier stages fall away, so too the thinking person does not regret the passing of the interests of old age. And when this happens, the fullness of life brings about the time which is ripe for death.

[77] I suppose I should explain my personal position on death. I seem to be able to clarify this better, the closer I come to the end of my life. You know, David, I knew your grandfather and, although we may have differed in our politics, he was a very distinguished American and dear to me. For me, he still lives; in fact, now after his death he lives the only type of life that can be counted as life. For as long as we are shut up in these frameworks of the body, we, of course, perform the certain functions and weighty tasks of human necessity. It is as if our heavenly spirit has been pressed downwards from its home on high and submerged, I suppose, into the earth, a condition opposite to its divine nature and to its eternity. But why do this? I believe God has sown spirits into human bodies in or-

der to create people who would work and take care of his earth and to create people who, in studying and thinking about the skies, that is about astronomy, science, and the higher things, would reflect these things in their steadfast way of life. I am led to this rather religious conclusion not only because it seems rational to me, but also because the great philosophers and the Bible teach something very similar.

[78] Look at Jefferson and the Deists. They have never doubted that we hold our spirits poured off from a divine and universal intellect. Socrates, the greatest of all philosophers, on his final day laid out much the same view of the immortality of the spirit. How should I add anything? But as I examine life and this world, I see such an incredible swiftness to the mind, so great a memory of the past and prediction of the future, so many talents, such great fields of knowledge, and so many discoveries, that I am convinced that whatever contains these gifts cannot be mortal. Think, too, that since the spirit, (or if you prefer, its abstract, "spirituality") is always in motion but does not have a prime or initial mover, and since therefore it moves itself, its motion will never end because it will not abandon itself. The spirit is also not made up of parts, there are no differing components in it: it is homogeneous and cannot be divided. If it cannot fall apart, it cannot die. The very fact that we are obviously born already

knowing many things, call it instinct if you will, is a powerful argument for the immortality of the human spirit. Little children learn difficult tasks and pick up so many talents so fast that they seem not to to be learning them for the first time but to somehow be remembering them. This is more or less my understanding from reading Plato.

[80] The honors paid to famous men after their deaths would not last if somehow their spirits did not live on as well. Their spirits may even actively help to keep their memory alive, I am not sure. But it doesn't make sense to me that the spirit should be alive when attached to a mortal body and then die when detached. In fact, it seems that at that point the spirit should actually be freer and maybe even purer and more conscious. It is obvious that all things in nature go back to where they came when they die. But we cannot see this directly with the spirit. Sleep might give us a hint – there seems to be nothing so similar to death as sleep. [81] When

51

we sleep, the spirit seems more released and freer from the body, and some say that in our dreams our spirit predicts the future. I don't know how much of this to accept, but that dreamy state which obviously does not operate totally according to the rules of our mortal minds may give us some hint that our spirit is also not dependent on the body. You don't need any of these ideas if you believe in God who rules the whole beautiful universe; he will keep our spirits alive with him. But if you are not a believer, they are worth thinking about.

[82] Let's be crassly realistic for a moment, if we may. Even your father and grandfather, David, and your father, Julie, along with other great Americans too numerous to list, did many of the important things they did for this country with at least one eye on how history would view them. The same is true for me, if you will let me toot my own horn a little, as old people are wont to do. Do you think that I would have worked so hard both in private life and in the Senate if I thought my reputation would end when my body gave up? This is another hint about the immortality of the spirit. If the future after we are dead had no relevance, our spirits in the here and now would give the future no thought and would not work so hard for it: we would simply enjoy a leisured life with no hassle and no competition. Somehow or other our spirits look forward to the times to come as if they will then live on after being released from the body. If that were not true, it seems

to me that the spirits of even the best men would not strive as they do, doing things that will be remembered when they are dead.

[83] One more thing about death and old age and then I will quit. It seems to me that the wisest of people, both religious and otherwise, die calmly, and that those who do not think carefully are the ones who die most reluctantly. Have you ever noticed that those spirits which think deeper and farther seem to be certain that they will set out for better things at death than the spirits of the duller blades? I am not sure what my spirit will do or be like after death, but it would be wonderful if I could meet your father and your grandfather and the other people I knew and respected while alive, along with all those characters I have only read about. Think about it. If that is the case, it will be hard to hold me back once the journey begins. And by the same token, if any miracle would grant me the chance to be a boy again and to cry in the nursery, I would certainly

refuse. There is no way I want to be recalled, as it were, from the finish line to the starting blocks now that I have run the whole race. [84] The death of my father made this clear to me. I am religious and I do long for the wonderful day when my spirit will see the people I have mentioned and especially my father without the hassle and pollution of this life. Never was there a finer man, never one more loyal to his family. I was at his funeral, and the thought that kept me going at that awful time was the conviction that our separation would not be a long one.

[85] I did go on a bit, but you were kind enough to ask. And now you know why my old age is not irksome but actually pleasant, something you, Julie and David, said you wondered at. I may be wrong in my belief in the immortality of the spirit: there are philosophers who think I am. I like my faith and I don't want to lose it. But anyway, if when I die my spirit also dies, I certainly won't give a flip about the opinions of dead philosophers. But seriously, even if there is nothing immortal about us, for each to die at the proper time is, of course, a desirable thing: as I have said, according to nature,

which puts limits to all life. Old age is the last act of the drama of life and when it is over we ought to leave it, especially if we have achieved a good fullness in it.

So, that's it. These were the things I wanted to say about old age. I hope you two young people live long enough to see in your own experience if what I have said tonight is true.

THE CAST OF CHARACTERS, ANCIENT AND MODERN

(My search for characters in American culture to replace Cicero's ancient Greeks and Romans found some matches that were humorous, some embarassingly stretched, but some amazingly parallel.)

The Interlocutors:

William **Fulbright** (1905-1995) replaces Marcus Porcius **Cato** (234-149 BC). Cicero made Cato the main speaker in his dialogue. Cato was the symbol of proper traditional Roman conduct and unflinching morality. He was born into a distinguished, but Plebian family and although he rose to hold all the high offices in the Roman state, he was famous for living simply, virtuously, and long. He was also a learned man, largely self-taught. As an old man, he began an enthusiastic reading of Greek philosophy. His obvious parallel in American culture is Abraham Lincoln. But Lincoln, although removed from us by only forty years or so more than Cato was removed from Cicero, seems to us

Americans to be too remote in our past to carry the sort of relevance Cicero achieved for Romans with his use of Cato.

Senator William Fulbright, on the other hand, was a powerful, respected and virtuous figure in our mid twentieth-century national history, a period we still remember and talk about, and so he got the part.

Dwight David **Eisenhower II** (b. 1948) replaces Publius Cornelius **Scipio Aemilianus** Africanus (Numantinus) (185-129 BC). Scipio was one of the young men Cicero made his secondary interlocutors along with Laelius, largely to act as foils to Cato and to set the fictitious historical scene for his dialogue. He was slightly younger than Laelius and came from one of Rome's most prestigious families, the Aemelians, and was adopted by another, the Cornelius Scipios. He had a distinguished military career, was elected head of state, and famous for the final distruction of Rome's ancient enemy, Carthage. He gathered around him a circle of literati largely known for their enthusiasm for Greek philosophy. He was 35 at the time of Cicero's dialogue.

David Eisenhower was 39 at the time of this fictitious

American dialogue. He is the grandson of President Dwight Eisenhower and son of John Eisenhower, onetime U.S. Ambassidor to Belgium. Mr. Eisenhower, although not echoing Scipio's political life, does reflect his Roman counterpart with his military, legal, educational, and literary careers. His grandfather named the presidential retreat, Camp David, after him.

Julie Nixon **Eisenhower** (b. 1948) replaces Gaius **Laelius** (Sapiens) (born ca. 188 BC). Laelius was the other of Cicero's secondary interlocutors. Cicero had been taught by one of Laelius' sons-in-law and thus he had a good source of information about the older man, whom he greatly admired. Laelius had a successful political career, largely due to the wealth and influence of his close friend, Scipio Aemelianus, Cicero's other secondary interlocutor. He was a member of Scipio's literary circle and was 38 at the time of the setting of Cicero's dialogue.

Mrs. Eisenhower was 39 at this fictitious dinner party with Senator Fulbright. Her family, although not as deep in pedigree as Laelius's, is like his in that it is of the highest political rank. She is a president's daughter and is married to a president's grandson. In her own right she has had a distinguished public and literary career. She staunchly defended her father during the Watergate scandal, often serving as the spokesperson for the Nixon family. She has been an editor for the *Saturday Evening Post*, written several books, and gone on to do important public service work. In the 2008 presidential campaign she donated significantly to the candidacy of Senator Barack Obama.

The Others:

*Charles **Atlas*** (1892-1972) replaces **Milo of Crotona** (late 500s BC). Milo was the proverbial ancient Greek strongman, winning the wrestling in the Olympic games six times and competing in them even after his fortieth birthday. Charles Atlas was the proverbial American strongman of the mid-twentieth century. He used clever advertising to market his successful body-building system. Milo is said to have carried an ox, the locomotive of its day, around a stadium; Atlas pulled an actual locomotive for 112 feet along its tracks.

*Irving **Berlin*** (1888-1989) replaces **Stesichorus** (ca. 630 - ca. 555 BC). Irving Berlin lived to be 101 and was still writing for Broadway when he was 72. His influence on American music and on the American musical theater has been immense. Stesichorus was an influential ancient Greek lyric poet who was supposedly blinded by Helen of Troy for some disparaging words he wrote about her. He later retracted his insults and regained his sight. He was famous for works written for the chorus. In fact, his name (actually a nickname) means "instructor of choruses." There is, I realize, a huge difference between the ancient Greek chorus and the Broadway one singular sensation, but the parallel was too good to pass up and so Irving Berlin got the part.

*Hugo **Black*** (1886-1971) replaces **Sextus Aelius** Paetus Catus (ca. 200 BC). Cicero uses Sextus Aelius as an example of someone who worked in intrepreting the law up to his final breath as an old man. Justice Black resigned from the U.S. Supreme Court in 1971 at age 85 because of ill health. He died eight days later.

*Gerry Curtis **Bridgeman*** (born 1971) replaces Titus Pomponius **Atticus** (109-32 BC). Cicero dedicated his book on old age to his best friend, Atticus. I replaced Atticus with my best friend, Curtis Bridgeman. The parallels are good but not perfect. Atticus was older than Cicero; Bridgeman is younger than me. Atticus was filthy rich; Bridgeman would like to be filthy rich. But both are loyal friends, cultivated gentlemen, avid readers, perceptive private commentators on politics, and learned in philosophy. Atticus was a nickname taken from the fact that he lived in Athens, a city in Attica and the intellectual center of the eastern Roman world. Bridgeman lives in Salem, Oregon, the intellectual center of, well, Salem, Oregon.

Winston Leonard Spencer **Churchill** (1874-1965) replaces Quintus **Fabius Maximu**s (ca. 280-203 BC). Fabius Maximus was a venerable Roman statesman, having been elected head of state five times. Cicero used him both because he was already at an advanced age (63) when he militarily saved the Romans from their most dangerous enemies, the Carthaginians, and because his whole life was a stirring example of the best of Roman leadership. Churchill was 66 when he led the British in their deadly struggle with Nazi Germany and he, like Fabius Maximus, had a truly inspiring career. He executed various important military and political roles for over fifty years, from his first election to Parliament in 1901 at age 26 to his retirement from the office of Prime Minister in 1955 when he was 80.

Congressmen *Dan* **Crane** (born 1936) and *Gerry* **Studds** (1937-2006) replace Lucius **Quinctius Flaminius** (early second century BC). Congressmen Crane and Stubbs were implicated in the sex scandal involving young congressional pages and were censured by the House in 1983. Crane lost the next election after the censure, but Gerry Studds, the first American national politician to be openly gay, went on to be relected six times. The word "Gerrymander" is partially coined from the name of his grandfather, Governor Gerry of Massachusetts. Lucius Quinctius Flaminius fell from even higher heights for his moral lapse. He had been a Roman admiral and elected head of state (consul) before his ejection from the Senate.

*Dwight David **Eisenhower*** (1890-1969) replaces **Lucius Paulus** (229-160 BC). Both General (later President) Eisenhower, our interlocuter's grandfather, and Lucius Paulus, the father of Cicero's interlocutor, Scipio, had distinguished military and political careers as senior citizens. By American standards, Paulus does not approach Eisenhower's impeccable morality, but both were national military heros and elected heads of state.

*Benjamin **Franklin*** (1706-1790) replaces **Xenophon** (431-355 BC). Franklin was anything but early to bed; he lived to be

84 and worked and wrote up to his last months. Some of his final works were important treatices advocating the abolition of slavery. His best seller was his yearly *Poor Richard's Almanack*, a collection of histories, seasonal weather data, hints for household and farming, along with his wit and famous aphorisms. Xenophon's career was as colorful and varied as Franklin's. He was a soldier, general, statesman, author, philosopher, and country gentleman. He was one of the rich young men who followed Socrates around, asking penetrating philosophical questions. Xenophon, like Franklin, wrote on many subjects, His *Oeconomicus*, was one of the ancient world's most famous manuals for successful household management and agriculture.

Robert **Frost** (1874-1963) replaces **Isocrates** (436-338 BC), whom Cicero uses as an example of an author who wrote significant works well into old age. Isocrates' subjects were rhetoric and political philosophy, and he is said to have committed suicide at age 98 in reaction to the news that King Phillip of Macedon had won a victory over the Greeks. Frost, on the other hand, was a great poet. But both showed remarkable productivity in their advanced years.

Mary Elizabeth **Frye** (1905-2004) replaces **Ennius** (ca 239-169 BC). Ennius was an early poet who wrote in Latin instead of the usual Greek. He lived earlier than did Cicero and was well known and immensely prolific. Cicero quotes him often, perhaps because his epic *The Annals* was a school text that Cicero had most likely studied as a boy. Unfortunately, little of his work survives. Mrs Frye, on the other hand, was virtually unknown as a poet until late in life when she admitted to having written the very popular "Do not stand at my grave and weep." The Dear Abby column corroborated her claim to its authorship.

Mohandas Karamchand **Gandhi** (1869-1948) replaces **Diogenes of Sinope** (412-323 BC). Ghandi is, of course, known universally for his non-violent means in obtaining political, individual, and spiritual independence for India. Although he was born to privilege, his strong convictions caused him to espouse a life with no material attachment. Diogenes, although never a great political leader like Ghandi, nonetheless attacked most of the social conventions of his day and became famous by living and preaching a life of total independence. His espoused life was so absurd to contemporaries that Plato dubbed him, "A Socrates gone mad."

Thomas Pryor **Gore** (1870-1949) replaces **Appius Claudius Caecus** (ca. 300 BC). Appius Claudius was the father of a political dynasty and accomplished many things in the high national offices he held, including administering the construction of the Appian Way and the Appian Aqueduct. He was appointed supreme military commander as an old man and totally blind. Senator Gore, the grandfather of the vice president, also founded a political dynasty and achieved a great deal helping the American farmer and the Native American. He too was a staunch tradtionalist, active until over 80, and, like Appius Claudius, totally blind.

William Franklin "Billy" **Graham, Jr.** (born 1918) replaces ***Gaius Gallus*** (mid-second century BC). Gallus was extremely famous among the Romans for study of the heavens; his passion for astronomy and writing astronomical works endured well into his old age. Billy Graham's passion for heaven catapulted him into international fame. He was one of the most influential Americans of the twentieth century and has continued his monumental evangelical work, speaking, preaching, and writing well into his 80s. He was a frequent guest in the White House and associated with all the presidents from Eisenhower to the younger Bush, with the exception of President Kennedy. President Obama paid him a visit at his home in North Carolina in 2010. He was particularly close to Richard Nixon.

Immanuel **Kant** (1724-1804) replaces **Plato** (429 347 BC). Plato, although not the first philosopher, is generally held to be the founder of Western philosophy and Kant, the founder of the discipline's modern stream. Plato is famous both for his rigorous method of philosophical inquiry and for his emphasis on the human or ethical importance of the subject. He wrote a great deal, usually in the form of a dialogue, and this became the standard form for written philosophical discourse. Immanuel Kant is usually mentioned in the same breath as Plato when discussing the great philosophers. He too exhibited rigor in his method and contributed much to the discipline of ethics, especially with his "categorical imperative," a complicated idea that stresses the motive for our right actions and its purity found in a universal imperative.

Nathan **Hale** (1755-1776) replaces Lucius Junius **Brutus** (late sixth century BC). In September of 1776 young Captain Hale (he was 21) was captured and executed as a spy by the British as he was noting their numbers, armaments, and positions on Long Island. His famous phrase, "I regret that I have but one life to lose for my country" has become a byword of dedication and patriotism from our founding fathers. Lucius Junius Brutus was one of the founding fathers of the Roman Republic and elected its first consul, or head of state. He is the distant ancestor of Marcus Brutus who helped assassinate Julius Caesar. Both Lucius Brutus and Nathan Hale fought to rid their homelands of the rule of kings and to establish elected government.

W. Averell **Harriman** (1891-1986) replaces **Themistocles** (524-459 BC). Themistocles came from common stock, but rose to be the most important Athenian national figure of his day. He advocated the shift to a strong naval position which allowed Athens to resist the second invasion of the Persians and go on to establish a huge maritime empire. His private life, however, was not beyond reproach.

Governor Harriman was an American national figure who ran in aristocratic circles. He was friends with the Roosevelts and married to former wives of members of the families of Winston Churchill and Cornelius Vanderbilt. He owned a stable of thoroughbred race horses. Among other offices, he served as governor of New York, US Ambassador to the Soviet Union and to Britain, US Secretary of Commerce, and Special Envoy to Europe in the wake of World War II. Although his private business dealings with German banks caused raised eyebrows, in his later years he was much respected as a senior American statesman.

Thomas Jefferson (1743-1826) replaces **Pythagoras** (ca. 570 - ca. 490 BC). Both the ancient Pathagoreans and the eighteenth-century Deists held that God was a superior intellect, a "universal reason," which set up the universe and established the laws which governed it. Pythagoras taught far more and far deeper things than our tenth-grade $A^2 + B^2 = C^2$. Obviously Jefferson's rather scientific God was the Christian one, while Pythagoras' was more of a mathematical construct.

Dr. Samuel Johnson (1709-1784) replaces **Architas of Tarentum** (late fifth century to mid fourth century BC). The oft-quoted Dr. Johnson, a college dropout, became the most important English literary figure of his age and is buried in Westminster

Abbey. He was a prolific author, essayist, poet, dramatist, critic, editor and lexicographer. His dictionary forms the basis of modern English usage and lexical precision. He contributed to and edited several popular London broadsheets, the predecessors of newspapers. Architas, a friend and contemporary of Plato, was one of the most famous Greek philosophers of his day, who, like Johnson, exerted lasting influence. He was most known as a mathematical philosopher. He saw the quality of life expressed in mathematical, musical, and moral harmony.

*John F. **Kennedy*** (1917-1963) makes a cameo appearance re-

placiing the Roman dramatist, **Caecilius Statius** (died ca. 168 BC): both talked about how people take actions to benefit the future even when they will not live long enough to be a part of it.

*Pope **Leo XIII*** (1810-1903, pope from 1878) replaces **Lucius Metellus** (ca. 290-221 BC). Leo XIII was an extremely old man for most of his long pontificate. He is credited with ushering the Church into the modern age and is much loved for his support of democratic institutions. Lucius Caecilius Metellus was most noted as a Roman general who fought against Carthage, learning how to thwart their dreaded war elephants. He was consul (head of state) twice and high priest (pontifex maximus) for the last twenty-two years of his long life. In the Roman system, the pontiff was not a life-long clergyman as the pope now is, but a statesman from a powerful family. The job carried temporary residence in a kind of White House, the Regia, situated in the Roman Forum. Even Julius Caesar was Pontifex Maximus.

John Marshall (1755-1835) replaces **Titus Coruncanius** (3rd century BC). Coruncanius was one of the first important professional Roman jurists. His teachings were influential in building the tradition of Roman law. Cicero uses him as an example of a senior jurist from a much earlier period. Chief Justice John Marshall, who did so much to establish the procedures and the importance of the U.S. Supreme Court in its early history, is the obvious American parallel. The famous crack in the Liberty Bell appeared when it was tolled at Marshall's funeral.

George S. McGovern (1922-2012) replaces **Spurius Postumius Albinus** (ca. 236-180 BC). Although Albinus did rise to become the Roman head of state, he died in his 50s, not that old even for an ancient Roman. As such, he was not really a fitting oldie to complain about old age's supposed lack of physical pleasure as Cicero's dialogue has him do. His lack of venerable years has caused one famous modern scholar to assume that Cicero simply grabbed the name of this rather obscure Roman politician from the official lists of Roman office-holders because it was written near to Cato's. But it was under Albinus' leadership that the Senate tried to suppress the wild rites of Bacchus at Rome. What better spokesman to complain about lack of physical pleasure? Tully, you earn points for subtle irony.

George McGovern was United States Senator from South Dakota from 1963 to 1981 and a major figure in American and international politics. He was the Democratic Party's nominee for president in 1972. He lost the election to Richard Nixon, but the Democrats' campaign headquarters was the object of the Watergate break-in and subsequent scandal. Both as senator and in his later years he was instrumental in establishing programs to promote nutrition and to fight world hunger.

Ethel **Merman** (1908-1984) replaces **Amblivius Turpio** (mid-second century BC). Amblivius Turpio led the most famous theatrical troupe of Cato's day. Ethel Merman was "the first lady of Broadway" throughout the middle decades of the twentieth century. When Rosalind Russell was given the movie part of Madame Rose, Merman's great Broadway role in the musical "Gypsy," Merman is said to have quipped: "There's a name for women like her, but it's seldom used in society outside a kennel."

Methuselah replaces **Arganthonius**, an ancient king who ruled in Cadiz, Spain in the sixth century BC. Cicero uses Arganthonius as the example of the longest living human he knew of; he supposedly lived to be 120. Our proverbial example of this is, of course, Methuselah, "Thus all the days of Methuselah were nine hundred and sixty-nine years; and he died." (Genesis, 5:27)

Glenn Miller (1904-1944) replaces Marcus Attilius **Regulus** (ca.

307-250 BC). Glenn Miller, an Iowa farm boy and college drop-out, went on to dominate the popular music charts in the late 1930s and early 40s. In 1943, at age 38, he was determined to join the Navy but turned down becaue of his age. He nonetheless persuaded the Army to allow him to enlist. His musical performances were an important part of maintiaining the morale of American troops in the middle years of World War II. On December 15, 1944 he boarded a single-engine plane to fly from England to Paris to entertain the troops. The plane was lost, and no trace has ever been found.

Regulus was the Romans' favorite example of someone who kept his promise even if it meant facing certain death. He was captured by Rome's great enemy, Carthage. He promised his captors that if they allowed him to go to

Rome to bargain for peace, he would return to Carthaginian captivity. He went to Rome, and kept his promise by returning to Carthage, where the Carthaginians executed him. According to one story, they killed him by removing his eyelids and then forcing him into bright sunlight.

Anna Mary Robertson (Grandma) **Moses** (1860-1961) replaces Leontinus **Gorgias** (487-376 BC). Cicero uses Gorgias as an example of an author who was creative in his extreme old age. He is credited with bringing the art of rhetoric from Sicily to mainland Greece. Grandma Moses did not start painting until she was 76 and went on to become one of America's most famous and beloved artists. Both lived to be over a hundred.

Thomas Phillip "Tip" **O'Neill** (1912-1994) replaces **Lucius Valerius Flaccus** (234-149 BC). O'Neill, the powerful and pyrotechnic Democratic Speaker of the U.S. House of Representatives, was a master at balancing the exigencies of old-line politics with strong moral conviction. He fought hard for the New Deal, championed universal health care in the 1970s, was a loud opponent of the Vietnam War, and an unwavering voice calling for the impeachment of Richard Nixon. He characterized the Reagan presidency as "a Christmas party for the rich." Valerius Flaccus was also a powerful figure in Roman politics. He was Cato's colleague as censor in 184 BC. The censors were the Roman officials who constructed the official lists of membership in the Roman Senate. Together they evicted Lucius Flamminius Quinctius from the Senate for having executed a defendant because a prostitute at a dinner party asked him to do it.

Charles H. Percy (1919-2011) replaces Gaius Livius **Salinator** (ca. 234-170 BC). Charles Percy lived to be 92 and enjoyed long and distinguished careers in American business and as senator from Illinois for eighteen years. He served as an officer in the US Navy during World War II. He was often in the national spotlight and twice contemplated running for president. Livius Salinator held many of the highest Roman naval and political posts, including the consulship twice. He was the founder and designer of Forum Livii, now the modern Italian city of Forli.

*Ronald **Reagan*** (1911-2004) replaces **Cyrus the Great** (ca. 600-530 BC). Ronald Wilson Reagan, the fortieth president of the United States, lived to be 97 and was already 75 at the time of our fictitious dinner party. Although not at all of Senator Fulbright's political persuasion, and often the brunt of jokes for falling asleep in important meetings, nonetheless in his confrontations with the Soviet Union, he spent much of his second term in an attempt to extend American influence abroad. Cyrus the Great was the king of Persia who within a single

decade put together the largest empire that part of the world had ever seen. This King of Kings long played a role in the lore of his subjects and of peoples, like the Greeks and Romans, who were not part of the Persian Empire.

Steve **Reeves** (1926-2000) replaces **Titus Pontius** (second cenury BC) the centurion. Cicero follows the Roman stereotype which considers centurions to be physically powerful men. Steve Reeves achieved his fame playing Hercules and similar muscle-bound characters in Hollywood movies of the 1950s and 60s.

William **Shakespeare** (1564-1616) replaces **Caecilius Statius** (ca. 200 - ca. 166 BC). Caecilius was a skillful adaptor of Greek plays into Latin and much quoted in Cicero's day. He lived at about the same time as did Cato, Cicero's principal interlocutor. Since he was a Gaul and had come to Rome as a war captive and thus a slave, he rose to literary prominence from even lower origins than did Shakespeare.

Alfred, Lord **Tennyson** (1809-1892) replaces Gnaeus **Naevius** (ca. 270-201 BC). Naevius was a Roman playwright with a poetic tongue that got him into trouble. Romans took their poetry seriously, and his satiric lines landed him in prison. He was famous for his play about the first Punic War, the Romans' death struggle with their rival empire of Carthage. Tennyson, the Victorian poet laureate, is cited by our generation almost as much as is Shakespeare, even if we have forgotten that it was Lord Alfred who penned our outmoded and pretentious quotes. "Theirs not to reason why, theirs but to do or die" and "It is better to have loved and lost than never to have loved at all" we owe to him. Tennyson was still writing poetry in his 80s.

James Strom Thurmond (1902-2003) replaces **Massinissa** (ca. 241-148 BC), king of Numidia (roughly northern modern Algeria) and famous for his vigor when over ninety. Senator Thurmond was in office when he was ten years older than even Massinissa. He was 100 when he resigned.

Earl Warren (1891-1974) replaces Publius **Licinius Crassus** Dives (born ca. 250 BC). Licinius Crassus had an important political career and was particularly noted for his command of Roman religious law, something he used in the political sphere during Rome's final struggle with Hannibal. Cicero uses him as an example of an active old man. Chief Justice Warren was active even after his retirement as leader of the famous Warren Commission investigating President Kennedy's assassination. The Warren Court is also noted for its use of judicial power in the executive sphere.

Comments on the Original Work, Cicero's *On Old Age* (*Cato Maior: De Senectute*)

Cicero was a lawyer – Rome's best – and he was obviously arguing a case in his *On Old Age*. He was not unaware of the disadvantages of being old, but his purpose in this work was to point out the advantages. Although he as a good lawyer leaves out arguments supporting the other side, he nonetheless admits he will do so in his very first paragraph: "There are problems in both our lives, as there are in all lives, but consolation (or maybe commiseration) is not what I have in mind here. This is a book about old age." Its upbeat ideas have struck a chord throughout the ages.

Cicero wrote his tract on old age in early 44 BC, probably before Caesar's assassination in mid March of that year. He was 62 when he wrote it, having achieved venerable years by Roman standards. He was not to enjoy much of his old age, however, for he would be killed by his great political enemy, Marc Antony, about a year later. With Caesar's control of the Roman government, Cicero was forced out of politics. He retired to the country to write. The *De Senectute* is one of a series of philosophical works he completed in his last years. He could have stayed safely in one of his country villas, enjoying the food, air, wine, gardens, and the leisure to write, but he didn't. In the wake of Caesar's death, Cicero was so incensed by actions of Antony, perceiving him to be an even greater danger to Roman liberty than Caesar had been, that he came out of retirement to deliver scathing speeches against Antony in the Roman Senate. To many, this is Cicero's finest hour: sacrificing his own old age by facing almost certain death at the hands of the new tyrant, an action taken at least in part because of his deep love for his country.

The work has been popular through the millenia. It was widely read by the ancient Romans themselves and has been translated into all the modern languages. It was printed very early in this country by none other than Benjamin Franklin. It was the first printing in America of any English translation of a classical work. Here is what Franklin, often shown with specs perched on his nose, said about it in his 1743 edition. Note that in 1743, Franklin was still a young man, age 37.

I have, Gentle Reader, as thou seest, printed this Piece of Cicero's in a large and fair Character, that those who begin to think on the Subject of OLD AGE, (which seldom happens till their Sight is somewhat impair'd by its Approaches) may not, in Reading, by the Pain small Letters give the Eyes, feel the Pleasure of the Mind in the least allayed.

Cicero's book was also much beloved by President John Adams. Today, there is even a Facebook page dedicated to it.

Suggestions for Further Reading

Boissier, Gaston, (Adnah David Jones, trans.) *Cicero and his Friends: A Study of Roman Society in the Time of Caesar*, 2nd ed. London: A. D. Jones and Co, 1897. (Reprint, New York: Cooper Square Publishers, 1970). [Bossier's work is nineteenth-century classical scholarship at its best. Jones' translation is extremely readable.]

Brown, Eugene, J. William Fulbright. *Advice and Dissent*. Iowa City: University of Iowa Press, 1985. [Brown does an excellent job of presenting Fulbright the man.]

Everitt, Anthony, *Cicero. The Life and Times of Rome's Greatest Politician*. New York: Random House, 2001. [This is a wonderful literary biography, that is, Everitt has with consummate skill joined and linked passages from Cicero's works together with the result that Cicero tells his own life's story.]

Falconer, W. A. (ed. and trans.), *Cicero XX De Senectute, De Amicitia, De Divinatione*. Cambridge, Massachusetts: Harvard University Press (Loeb Classical Library), 1979. [This is a sound edition and perceptive translation. The Loeb Classical Library presents their volumes with the Latin on left-hand page and the English translation conveniently printed on the facing right-hand page.]

Harris, Robert, *Imperium*. New York: Pocket Books, 2006. [A well-written historical novel about Cicero's election campaign for the consulate in 64 B.C. It provides insight into the complexities of Roman politics in the engaging way that good historical novels do.]

Lacy, W. K., *Cicero and the End of the Roman Republic.* London: Holder and Stoughton, 1978. [Lacy is particularly perceptive with Cicero's personality, both with his public one as politician and lawyer and in his private life.]

Powell, J. G. F., *Cicero: Cato Maior de Senectute.* New York: Cambridge University Press, 1988. [This masterly edition and commentary on Cicero's *De Senectute* is a product of deep erudition, sensitivity, and sound judgement. No serious scholarly work on the subject should be without it.]

Thayer, Bill (ed.) For those who prefer computers to books, Falconer's Loeb translation (see above) has been put on the net by Bill Thayer along with helpful links to the Latin text and other translations into modern languages: http://penelope.uchicago.edu/Thayer/E/Roman/Texts/Cicero/Cato_Maior_de_Senectute/text*.html

Woods, Randall Bennett, *Fulbright: A Biography.* Cambridge University Press, 1995. [Woods has produced a sensitive, complete, balanced, soundly scholarly yet thoroughly readable biography of the senator.]

ABOUT THE AUTHORS

Richard Gerberding has recently retired as Professor of History and Director of Classical Studies from the University of Alabama in Huntsville. He currently lives in Oregon where he enjoys reading, teaching Latin, and dinner.

Lance Rossi resides in Salem, Oregon, where he enjoys gardening, drawing, and learning what dead (and living) people have to say about the world.

Marcus Tullius Cicero died in 43 BC and would not be surprised at all that his ideas on old age were still being read some two thousand years later and some fifteen hundred years after the empire which he once led disappeared from the map.

qp

Visit us at *www.quidprobooks.com.*